T0146653

8 STEPS TO GETTING ANYTHING YOU WANT IN LIFE

THE POWER OF GOD, YOUR THOUGHTS, AND THE UNIVERSE

PRINCESS ELLIS

WESTBOW PRESS®

A DIVISION OF THOMAS NELSON & ZONDERVAN

Scripture quotations marked (NIV) are taken from the Holy Bible, New International Version®,
NIV®. Copyright © 1973, 1978, 1984, 2011 by Biblica, Inc.™ Used by permission of Zondervan.
All rights reserved worldwide. www.zondervan.com The "NIV" and "New International Version"
are trademarks registered in the United States Patent and Trademark Office by Biblica, Inc.™

Scripture quotations taken from the New American Standard Bible® (NASB), Copyright ©
1960, 1962, 1963, 1968, 1971, 1972, 1973, 1975, 1977, 1995 by The Lockman Foundation
Used by permission. www.Lockman.org

WestBow Press books may be ordered through booksellers or by contacting:

WestBow Press
A Division of Thomas Nelson & Zondervan
1663 Liberty Drive
Bloomington, IN 47403
www.westbowpress.com
1 (866) 928-1240

ISBN: 978-1-5127-9446-5 (sc)
ISBN: 978-1-5127-9445-8 (e)

Library of Congress Control Number: 2017910943

Print information available on the last page.

WestBow Press rev. date: 07/24/2017

Contents

Acknowledgement

I want to take this opportunity, to say an immense Thank You, to Dannella Barnett, for all your encouraging words, and your dedicated assistance in being my "proof reader" and "sounding board" for this project.

Your continued feedback was invaluable to this entire process, and your enthusiasm and appetite for more, gave me additional drive to complete this book.

For this, and for being my very dear friend, I am truly, truly, grateful.

Also, to all my friends, who played the part of Pilot Readers, thank you so much for taking the time out of your busy lives, to read through, and provide feedback for this book. Your time and effort was greatly appreciated.

Introduction

This book was written with the intention for it to become a Life Manual for my friends, and by extension, the general public, as the concepts that it teaches, will not only change your Life, but also your Reality.

These are concepts that I live by, and I found that my friends were always asking me questions like, "How do you stay so positive?" or "How is it that things always seem to work out for you?"As such, I proceeded to try and teach them these concepts, but found that they had difficulty remembering each step, and just how to go about this process of Mental Reprogramming.

Therefore, in an effort to make it easier for them, I decided that instead of trying to tell them repeatedly, I would just write it down. By doing that, they would constantly have a sort of Manual with them, to refer to whenever they needed to; whenever they forgot a step; or whenever they just needed reminding, of the Power their thoughts have over their reality.

And so was born, this book.

My Blueprint, for Life!

STEP 1

Understand God's Absolute Control

"I pray that the eyes of your heart may be enlightened in order that you may know the hope to which he has called you, the riches of his glorious inheritance in his holy people, 19 and his incomparably great power for us who believe. That power is the same as the mighty strength 20 he exerted when he raised Christ from the dead and seated him at his right hand in the heavenly realms, 21 far above all rule and authority, power and dominion, and every name that is invoked, not only in the present age but also in the one to come." Ephesians 1:18-21 [NIV]

The first, and most fundamental truth you need to realize and accept, in this entire concept, is that God, and **only** God, controls the Universe, and ALL that is in it!

As is written above, God's Power is *"far above all rule and authority, power and dominion, and every name that is invoked, not only in the present age but also in the one to come"*. This is a very Literal truth, which means exactly what it says; there is no one on earth, nor has there ever been, nor will there ever be, anyone, who has more Power and Authority, than God.

Therefore, as Humans, we need to Know this, and Understand this, and place this knowledge at the forefront of our every thought, so that every other thought, falls below this one.

What this will then mean, is that we will no longer see circumstances, or obstacles, or trials, from the viewpoint as if they are on the same level as us; or worse, see them as bigger than us, and hence insurmountable. We will, as of now, banish this false viewpoint. And instead, replace it with the truth. The truth that God is Above ALL things! All trials, all circumstances, all possibilities, all desires, all dreams, all goals.

Anything you want in this world, God is in control of it, and therefore, God is the **only** one, capable of giving it to you.

So with the changing of your mental viewpoint, you have now seated God in his rightful place, as the Head of Everything, with everything below him, and under his complete control. Make a mental picture of this, and keep it constantly for reference. It will help you to keep this truth ever present and constant in your mind.

So, the basic idea of this Step is, Understanding that: God created all things; God controls all things; God can grant you all things; Nothing happens in this world that God does not ordain; And, there is nothing that Man can do, to stop anything that God ordains, for You.

All you need to do, is Believe!

Step 2

Understanding the Power of the Universe

"Do not defile yourselves in any of these ways, because this is how the nations that I am going to drive out before you became defiled. 25 Even the land was defiled; so I punished it for its sin, and the land vomited out its inhabitants. 26 But you must keep my decrees and my laws. The native-born and the foreigners residing among you must not do any of these detestable things, 27 for all these things were done by the people who lived in the land before you, and the land became defiled. 28 And if you defile the land, it will vomit you out as it vomited out the nations that were before you." Leviticus 18:24-28 [NIV]

God gave Power to the Universe!

When God created everything, he bestowed Power to certain things in his creation. **He gave Power to the Lion and made it King of the jungle. He gave Power to the Eagle and made it the most magnificent of birds. He gave Power to the Universe, to Act, within the boundaries already set by Him.** And lastly, He gave Power to Mankind, to Rule and have Dominion over, EVERYTHING else that he had created! However, we will discuss more about Mankind's Power when we get to Step 6. In this Step, we will discuss the Power that God gave to the Universe.

Now, before we can understand this concept, we must first understand, that when God made creation, **only** Mankind, was given Cognitive Understanding and Advanced Mental Processing to the level that we (Humans) have it. Mankind is also the only thing within creation that God decided to give the gift of Free Will. Nothing else within creation was given this unique gift. What this therefore means, is that Everything else within creation, Animals; Nature; The Universe; are all under God's complete Sovereignty. So they do not have the Power to disobey God, or to say No, or to act outside of God's accordance. They are not able to think, and to decide, that they will misuse the Power that God has given them. Therefore, God was able to give them Power, as He wishes, and set the boundaries of this Power, without any reservations.

When we understand this foundation, we can then begin to fathom the statement made above.. *He gave Power to the Universe, to Act, within the boundaries already set by Him*. What we are saying here, is that the Universe was given the Power to ACT, whenever it is **Activated** to do so, once it is within the boundaries, that were set out by God. Note, that in the scripture quoted above, the Lord said.. "*And if you defile the land, it will vomit you out as it vomited out the nations that were before you*." The Lord stated it this way on purpose. If you read the Old Testament you will see, that God isn't anything, if not detailed! Extremely, infinitely, detailed. Therefore, He chooses his words very specifically. And this statement is no different. What God was saying here, is that He has already given Power to the

Land, so that whatever should defile it, based on His Rules and His Order, the Land has within it, the Power, to vomit out its inhabitants. Now, in a literal sense, this could refer to Natural Disasters, such as Earthquakes, or Floods, or any other such natural disaster. But the important thing to note, is that the inhabitants of the land, were no more.

Similarly, God gave Power to the Universe, to Act when it is activated to do so; and as Humans, WE have the Power, to Activate, the Universe! With our thoughts. With our Spoken words. We Speak; We Think; and the Universe responds, by bringing into our path, that which we have thought, or spoken; for God, made it so.

However, as Humans, we tend to just go through life, **not** being constantly, consciously, aware of this fact; and as such, we Think and Speak, all manner of things, and in so doing, we Activate the Universe, to bring these things into our path, most times, without meaning to do so.

Therefore, what we want to do in this Step, is become constantly aware of this truth. In that, we will now begin to Think, and Speak, **only** the things we **want** the Universe to bring to us! We will recognize, that our thoughts, and our words have Power, and whatever we speak, and think, we are basically asking the Universe for. After recognizing this, we will then start to **Ask** for what we **want**, and know, and most importantly, **expect**, that the Universe will bring to us what we have asked for.

The most important thing to remember in this Step is that; The Universe gives you what you **Expect**, **NOT**, what you **Want**. Therefore, if you ask the Universe for something that you Want, but then don't Expect that it will happen, then it won't! That, is the Power of Doubt; which we will discuss in Step 7.

The Universe has the Power within it, to bring you, Anything you want; all you have to do, is Ask, and *Believe*!

Step 3

Rising Above your Human Psyche

"Jesus looked at them and said, "With man this is impossible, but not with God; all things are possible with God." Mark 10:27 [NIV]

NOTHING is impossible with God!

This statement, is the foundation of this step. Stop giving Power to Mankind!

As Humans, in our lack of understanding of the Universe, and how it works, we will naturally see things from a Human perspective. This is based on years of conditioning, through Education, Social Behaviour Norms, and General Knowledge of how the world works. So we go through the world, and through life, accepting, adopting, and believing this way of thinking, because it is innate, and it is what we know.

So, for example, we know that, the person in charge of giving us a promotion at work, is our boss or our manager; we know that, the person in charge of giving us a visa, is the consular at the embassy; we know that, the unit in charge of our fate if we break the law, is the judge/jury and by extension the government; we know that, if we choose the wrong answers on an exam, we will not pass; we know that our boss is in charge of the decision to fire us from a job; we know that if we are diagnosed with a terminal illness, we will die; and we know that if the doctor has pronounced us dead, then we can't come back to life—right?

Wrong!

As we discussed in the first step, God is the only one who is in control of everything!

So in this step, we want to challenge you to stop thinking naturally and start thinking supernaturally. What this means is that we will stop looking at things from our natural human perspective and instead start looking at everything from a supernatural perspective. This refers to everything in life! It requires a complete mental reconditioning. One in which, we make God the only person in control of anything in our lives. Any decision, any outcome, any prospect. Anything on Earth that you have been taught is under the control of a Human being, or is within their authority, that is wrong. It's that simple. Humans control nothing. God controls everything. So take All your wants to Him; all your troubles. Understand that God has the Power to change **Any** situation.

So let us revisit the list above, under the Supernatural way of thinking. The one responsible for allowing us to get a promotion at work, is God. The one responsible for us getting a visa, is God. The one responsible for our fate if we break the law, is God. Even with choosing the wrong answers on an exam we can pass, with God's intervention. The one responsible for the decision in us being fired from a job, is God.

God can heal us from any terminal illness. And God can certainly, raise us from the state of death. We only need but to trust in his Sovereign Power, and place him above all things. Because the flip side of this truth is, if you give Mankind the Power, by **mentally** placing them in charge of the things in your life, then alas, you have just given them the Power, in **reality**!

Growing up, I have always been taught, that when it's your time, it's your time. That every man has an appointment with death. And that when that day comes, there is nothing that you can do to prevent it.

This is another Absolute that we are taught in life. That we accept as fact; and the hard reality; because, God has made it so.

Therefore, who would ever think, or even dream, of asking God for an extension on your life.., when God himself has told you, that it was now your time to die …

That, would be unheard of!! Right..?

"In those days Hezekiah became ill and was at the point of death. The prophet Isaiah son of Amoz went to him and said, "This is what the LORD says: ***Put your house in order, because you are going to die****; you will not recover." [2] Hezekiah turned his face to the wall and prayed to the LORD,[3] "Remember, LORD, how I have walked before you faithfully and with wholehearted devotion and have done what is good in your eyes."*

And Hezekiah wept bitterly.[4] Before Isaiah had left the middle court, the word of the LORD came to him: [5] "Go back and tell Hezekiah, the ruler of my people, 'This is what the LORD, the God of your father David, says: I have heard your prayer and seen your tears; I will heal you. On the third day from now you will go up to the temple of the LORD. ⁶ ***I will add fifteen years to your life****." 2 Kings 20:1-6 NIV*

Now what do you note most in the verse above?

The fact that Hezekiah's life was at an end, by God's own will and command? The fact that Hezekiah believed enough, to think that his Praying and weeping before the Lord, because he was not ready to die as yet, may make a difference? The fact that he was "crazy" enough to Hope, that God would change his mind? Or, if you are like me, was it the fact, that God, actually, granted his desire, and Extended His Life??

This verse, goes against so many things that we have been taught to believe as humans, about how the world works, and how life works, and even, about how God works.

But I believe, that this verse proves, without a shadow of a doubt, that we, know Nothing, about how God works. That we limit God with our everyday Human way of thinking.

And that we don't **mentally**, allow God the space, and room He needs, in order to work Miracles in our lives.

So know this:

The day we stop limiting God, is the day we will start achieving, the ***Impossible!***

Step 4

God WANTS to give you your Heart's Desires

*"But seek first his kingdom and his righteousness, and **all** these things will be given to you as well." Matthew 6:33 [NIV]*

God already gave us the Key!

As Humans, we tend to go through life, constantly trying to find, the Key. We embark upon an endless search, of trying to find that one thing.., that will make us Rich; that will make us successful; that will make us finally achieve the big house and the expensive car; that will make us live lavishly and comfortably in life; that will make us want for nothing; that will give us the ability to be truly happy; that thing, that will make ALL our dreams come true!

As Humans, we go through life, missing the thing that has been there, right before our very eyes, from the beginning of time. We go through life missing it, because we are searching everywhere *else*, to find it. But the answer you are looking for, cannot be found anywhere else. Because, the answer, is here:

*²⁵ "Therefore I tell you, do not worry about your life, what you will eat or drink; or about your body, what you will wear. Is not life more than food, and the body more than clothes? ²⁶ Look at the birds of the air; they do not sow or reap or store away in barns, and yet your heavenly Father feeds them. Are you not much more valuable than they? ²⁷ Can any one of you by worrying add a single hour to your life? ²⁸ "And why do you worry about clothes? See how the flowers of the field grow. They do not labor or spin. ²⁹ Yet I tell you that not even Solomon in all his splendor was dressed like one of these. ³⁰ If that is how God clothes the grass of the field, which is here today and tomorrow is thrown into the fire, will he not much more clothe you—you of little faith? ³¹ So do not worry, saying, 'What shall we eat?' or 'What shall we drink?' or 'What shall we wear?' ³² **For the pagans run after all these things,** and your heavenly Father knows that you need them. ³³ **But seek first his kingdom and his righteousness, and all these things will be given to you as well."** Mathew 6:25-34 NIV*

Do you understand the magnitude of this scripture!!??

God is telling you, that He knows all the things you want, and all the things you need. The trivial things we as Humans worry about everyday.., food, clothes, shelter, etc, etc.. God is telling you, that He knows that you need these things, and that he will give them to you freely. You wouldn't even have to Ask for them! All you have to do, is forget about all the things that you want, and need, just forget about them and do one thing..

Seek. God. FIRST!

Not after you have tried everything else and they have failed. Which they will. That, is the Hard way.

But there is a much easier way, to access everything you've ever wanted, dreamt of, or hoped for. That way, is God. The creator, ruler, and owner, of All things. The Only one, that can give you Everything, along with a peace of mind, true contentment, and salvation for your soul. What more could any Human ask for?

So in this chapter, we want to challenge you. Seek God today. Give your life to Him, today. Accept Him in your heart, today. And then feel free to start testing Him at His word. Because He will, deliver on his promises.

So the basic idea of this step is, God has made a bargain with you, to seek Him First; to give your life to Him, and He will give you Everything. So as Humans, all we have to do, is keep our end of the bargain, and then request for God to keep His.

He will!

Step 5

Asking for what you want

"Take delight in the LORD, and he will give you the desires of your heart." Psalm 37:4 [NIV]

The Meat of the Matter!

Now that you have properly adjusted your mindset by going through the other steps, you are now ready to learn, to **"Ask for what you want"**. Literally!

This is where we begin, to put all that we now believe, into Practice.

As the verse states above, "Take delight in the Lord"- (this is what we have been covering in the past 4 steps), and it goes on to say.. "And He will give you, the desires of your heart"; we will therefore learn now, how to ask for those desires; of the Lord; and of The Universe.

So what have we learnt so far?

That God controls everything. That God gave Power to the Universe. That God gave Humans the Power to Activate The Universe. That God wants to give you your desires. And that all you have to do is Ask and Believe.

Don't be afraid to Ask!

Though God knows what is in your heart, you need to Voice your desires out loud.

Speak them to the Universe. And expect them to be realized.

As Humans, we constantly have a multitude of thoughts and wishes and desires running through our minds and rested within our hearts, which God is aware of. However, those desires are usually being changed and adjusted just as rapidly as they come to us. This is why it is so important to Voice a specific desire out loud if you want it to be brought into your path, and hence realized.

You will also need to be very specific in the request you are making, as the Universe does not have the Power to think for itself, and hence, cannot make sense of a jumbled desire or wish. So you need to learn to Ask for exactly what it is you want.

Therefore, you can't just say, "I would like a job", and then when you are offered a Housekeeping job, you complain that, that's not the job you wanted. After all, you only asked for "a job", nothing specific. So, the Universe will grant you your wish, just as generally.

Ask for what you want!

Don't just say, "I want a promotion", or "I want a car", or "I want a husband/wife".., if you want something specific, then be just as specific or detailed with your request.

** I wanted to move out of my family home, but I wanted an apartment with some very specific features. I wanted a 1 Bedroom Apartment, in a gated complex, with 24hr security, fully furnished, with hot and cold water, a laundry room with washers and dryers, for an affordable cost, which included utilities …

This is what I sent out into the Universe, and this is what I focused on, and envisioned myself living in.. And Alas! I got Exactly what I asked for! With even some extra features to boot, like free Wifi!

What is even more Amazing, is that I don't meet the usual requirements that persons need to have in order to be considered for an Apartment on this Property, and there is a waiting list with hundreds of other qualified persons.. However, when God is on your side, and you are operating under Divine Favour, then none of those things matter. You just need to Ask for it, and it will be yours! Against all odds. **

So say to the Universe, "Universe, I want to meet this person", or "I would like tickets to this concert", or "I would like a job at this company", or "I want a free ride to work".. there is No Limit to what you can ask for!

Because, God controls Everything, and the Universe is Bigger than Everything, and God has Every Resource at his disposal, to grant you Anything, that you desire!

Princess Ellis

Amazing isn't it?

> *"Now to him who is able to do immeasurably more than all we ask or imagine, according to his power that is at work within us." (Ephesians 3:20) [NIV]*

Let God be Praised!

Step 6

COMMAND your Universe

"He replied, Because you have so little faith. Truly I tell you, if you have faith as small as a mustard seed, you can say to this mountain, 'Move from here to there,' and it will move. Nothing will be impossible for you." Matthew 17:20 [NIV]

You Have the Power!

God made the Universe, and gave to it, it's Power. Then God created Man, and gave us Dominion over Everything else that he created. *"You made them a little lower than the angels; you crowned them with glory and honor and put everything under their feet." Hebrews 2:7-8 [NIV]* This means, that We-Humans, have been given Dominion over the Universe, by God himself. Which means, that We, have the Power to **Command** the Universe, and the Universe in turn, **Must** Respond.

Do you understand the magnitude of this fact..?

Take a moment to read, and absorb, the bible verse quoted above.

"Truly I tell you, if you have faith as small as a mustard seed, you can say to this mountain, 'Move from here to there,' and it will move."

Command your Universe!

I will share an experience with you:

Recently, I had a situation, which required for me to speak with a particular person. However, I had no contact for her, as we were just mere acquaintances. So I had no phone number, no email, no contact for anyone who may have her information, nothing. So, I decided to call upon the Universe, for assistance. This was a Thursday. I said to the Universe "Universe, I need you to bring me -person's name-, as I need to speak with her urgently". From the moment I spoke that into the Universe, I started expecting that I would run into her. I walked around with that expectation, and kept speaking it to the Universe. When Thursday ended and Friday came and I hadn't run into her as yet, I said "Universe, what's up? Why haven't I seen her yet? I need to talk to her." And again, I went about expecting that I would see her somewhere. Now, for some reason, I expected that I would run into her in the vicinity I thought she might have reason to be, which is also somewhere that I frequented, so my sense of expectation was more heightened when I was in this vicinity. However, on Saturday, (2 days after making this request of the Universe), I was seated outside a fast food restaurant, and there she was, walking by!

Coincidence?

There is no such thing as coincidence.

I spoke. I believed. I expected. And it manifested.

Why was I able to make this request, and have absolute faith that it would happen?

When you begin to understand, and process the fact, that the Universe, is much bigger than you and I can ever imagine, and that God has Every resource at his disposal, then you can begin to fathom how I could request this and not doubt its possibility.

To do this, you must enlarge your vision, to way above what you are able to see in your limited view of the world.

The Universe, is your ultimate resource. Holding within it, the ability, the Power, to bring in your path Anything you can ever wish for, as it's resources are Limitless. It is not restricted, by rules, or laws, or land mass, or continents, or anything that could ever limit you or I. It's capabilities are unbounded.

So go ahead, and *Dream*.

Wish.

Desire.

Princess Ellis

Ask.

Believe.

Expect.

And it shall be Manifested!

Step 7

The Power of Positive Thinking

"Have faith in God," Jesus answered. [23] "Truly I tell you, if anyone says to this mountain, 'Go, throw yourself into the sea,' and does not doubt in their heart but believes that what they say will happen, it will be done for them." Mark 11:22-23 [NIV]

Doubt kills your dreams before they even start!

Why do you doubt?

Let's retract.., you Know that God created Everything, you Know that God has ultimate Power over Everything, you Know that God can Do Anything, and that Nothing is Impossible with God.. right?

Then why do you doubt?

Do you realize that when you Doubt, you are essentially saying, that you don't believe that God can grant you whatever it is you are doubting will happen..? Which in turn means, that you don't Trust God! Yes, that is exactly what it means.

You either Trust that God can do it, or you don't. In which case, you Doubt that God can do it!

Therefore, the first thing you need to do in this Step, is decide which side you are on. You are either on the side of God, or on the side of Doubt.

But Know, that the two CANNOT exist in the same space. It's either one, or the other.

Now, once you are on the side of God, there is NOTHING but Positivity!

You will consistently have an outlook of Anything being possible with God, never Doubting for a moment the possibility of whatever you are asking, or praying for, or imagining. Instead, you will exist with a constant knowledge that No Task or Wish or Desire is too great for God to deliver.

Jesus said so himself.. *"**Have faith in God**," ... if anyone says to this mountain, 'Go, throw yourself into the sea,' **and does not doubt in their heart** but believes that what they say will happen, it will be done for them."*

Tap into the Power that God has given you!

Speak what you desire, and Don't Doubt that it will happen, but Believe!

Clear you mind of all Doubt and Negativity. Understand that you are operating under God's Divine Power. Then Speak your desires into the Universe, and watch them be Manifested.

That is the Power of God within you!

Positivity is more than just a thought, it is an entire Outlook on life, which is constant and consistent. You may be thinking that it is difficult to stay positive with so much Negativity happening around us all the time, however, it is not difficult at all. Once your perspective has been adjusted to place God above all things, and you have ultimate trust in him, and his Power over Everything, then, being positive becomes easy.

You also need to understand, that Negative thoughts attract Negative things into your life, while Positive thoughts will attract Positive things. This is a Fact. The choice is yours.

When you speak a desire into the Universe, when you pray for something that you want to happen, Positive thoughts and Positive energy is the food that fuels those desires until they are Manifested.

The moment you start doubting and start infusing your desires with Negative energy, you just killed its Manifestation.

When Positive thoughts and Negative thoughts are battling in your mind, you are only hurting your dreams and desires, as where Positivity fuels dreams, Negativity poisons them.

So keep a mental image of the war you are creating within yourself, within your world, while remembering how this will affect your desires.

So in this step we want you to constantly keep this in your mind. Understand the role that Negative thoughts and Doubting play in your dreams remaining Unfulfilled. Then decide if you want to continue having a Negative outlook.

** I found myself in a spot recently where several bills were piling up on me, creating a mountain that I couldn't see beyond. College tuition would be due shortly, credit cards were maxed, there was a personal loan I was repaying, car insurance would be due in a few weeks, plus rent and food, and I had an upcoming engagement overseas..

I went over my budget countless times, trying as best as I can to see my way out. However, no matter how or where I cut down, it still didn't look like I would make a dent in these bills. Still, I just kept remaining positive about it, and thinking, something must come through, and that it would be okay. I would pay off the bills eventually, plus I was expecting a promotion at work for a position I had been Acting in for a few months, so I kept hoping I would get it in time to help with some of the bills. We were in August, and most of the bills would be due in September. Hence I kept silently praying that I would receive the promotion by September, and then everything would be okay.

I intended to use my final paycheck in August to start paying on some of them, with the hopes that, in September, I would be better able to cover them all.

Now when our final paycheck arrived in August, imagine my total shock and surprise, when I saw that my pay was doubled! When I inquired whether this was an error, I was advised by my Boss that she had decided to give me a special commission for Acting in that same position! Needless to say, I was able to make a significant dent in my bills, and I had done nothing, but trusted God and continued to think Positive! **

"But when you ask, you must believe and not doubt, because the one who doubts is like a wave of the sea, blown and tossed by the wind. That person should not expect to receive anything from the Lord. Such a person is double-minded and unstable in all they do." -James 1-:6-8[NIV]

Step 8

Thinking it into Being

"Therefore I tell you, whatever you ask for in prayer, believe that you have received it, and it will be yours." Mark 11:24 [NIV]

The Power of Visualization!

This is, the Icing on the cake. The Ultimate step, in achieving your dreams, and your goals.

A Step, that when mastered, will have you seeing results so quickly, it will be Uncanny!

Learn to Visualize your goals!

When you have decided on a goal, the mental work, is equally, or even **more** important, than the physical work. You need to immediately start mentally charting your course to getting to that goal, and constantly, visualizing achieving it. While you continue to do the physical work required to get there.

To reference a previous example, when I decided that I wanted to move out, I obviously started looking for a place.. However, I also immediately, started visualizing the place that I wanted. Constantly thinking about it over and over in my mind.

What it would be like moving in; how I would feel when I'm there; how happy I would be to have my own space; how great it will be to have all the amenities I wanted; the sense of freedom and independence I would have.. Just everything! This was the constant image in my mind, that I fostered every day, until the day, I actually moved in- **1 month**, after setting this goal!

This is what you need to do with All your goals, until they are realized.

Visualize. Visualize. Visualize.

When you have mastered this Step, the Universe will begin to manifest your desires, seemingly, out of nowhere!

At this stage, you will but have to think of someone, for them to appear, or make contact with you somehow. Alot of times, without you even intending to do so.

But you will be so infused with God's Power and Positive Energy, that you don't even have to speak your desires to the Universe anymore, because one simple thought, will result in their manifestation!

At this stage, you will no longer doubt that anything is possible, based on all the experiences you will have of your thoughts and desires being realized, once you start following these steps.

Therefore, **with doubt removed**, you have now created room, for ALL your desires to be manifested, **automatically!**

> *"Therefore I tell you, whatever you ask for in prayer, **believe that you have received it**, and it will be yours."*

As stated in the Bible verse above, the Power lies in, you having **Absolute** belief, that anything you ask for **Will**, be granted.

That is the Key!

Right now, I am visualizing completing this book, and having hundreds of copies printed. I'm visualizing being able to give copies to my friends and acquaintances whom I believe it will benefit. I'm visualizing my book being distributed across churches islandwide. I'm visualizing being asked to do interviews regarding this book and the ideas that it proposes. I'm visualizing the impact it will have on the masses as persons begin to read it and start following the steps. I'm visualizing it becoming a worldwide sensation, and touching the lives of many people. I'm visualizing being offered a PhD in Psychology, based on the widespread success this book will have, in accomplishing Mental Reprogramming

- Jan. 3, 2017 –

"The LORD said to Moses, "Is the LORD'S power limited? Now you shall see whether My word will come true for you or not."

-Numbers 11:23 [NASV]

"Now to him who is able to do immeasurably more than all we ask or imagine, according to his power that is at work within us"

-Ephesians 3:20 [NIV]

About the Author

Princess Ellis is the CEO of 2 Wild Entertainment, an Event Planning, and Talent Management company. She is the creator and organizer of, gospel concert series "The Power of Praise", and also, the founding member of Gospel Duo-Sisters in Harmony, which she formed with a long time friend in 2012. It is her intention, to make "The Power of Praise" an Annual concert, and a signature one on the yearly Calendar of events. She also plans on releasing music from her duo, later this year. Princess is currently pursuing her BSc. in Psychology, and intends to open a Practice someday, in order to further fulfill her passion of helping people. This is her first book.

Printed in the United States
By Bookmasters